BORN TO LOVE

By Suzi B

Everything is achieved through Love.

View life in the eyes of Love.

SELF-LOVE is the action you take when prioritising your wellness without compromise, honouring the life YOU want to live.

BORN TO LOVE ~ ALWAYS!

Live in the light of Love.

Suzi B xxx

Foreword

Positively navigating life with love

Hello my darlings,

I want to share with you how you can get the most out of this book and how you can use love to help you positively navigate any change needed in your life.

Do you know that something needs to change but sure not what it is or where to start? Or do you struggle with change generally? Do you feel mentally and emotionally stuck, trapped in toxic or negative relationships, anxious or overwhelmed? Are you prone to self-sabotage? Do you think that something may be lacking? Are you stuck because of a past event or trauma? Are you fearful of the future?

Do you want to make big changes, reset your life, change your relationships, or career and gain powerful life changing results in your business or private life?

If you answered yes to any of the above, I want you to know that you are not alone. It is possible to change, to clear the past, to heal, to trust and love yourself and to get more of what you want in life.

My mission is to change modern world values by sharing with you simple yet powerful methods of facilitating change within the pages of this book. These methods will help you stay calm and positive, and boost your emotional and mental resilience, helping you thrive to achieve more of what you want in life.

I have over 20 year's experience as a life coach and mentor, and I am qualified in Neuro-Linguistic Programming (NLP), hypnotherapy and mindfulness, all powerful ways of making what you want in life happen.

I use these techniques and strategies in this book. Born to Love helps guide you through the transition of internal to external love. As you start to confidently change and effortlessly shift your thoughts, empowering you to expand your passion to give satisfaction, enrichment and allowing you to positively connect more towards your meaning of life.

From a very young age and through all life's complications and challenges, I chose love. This helped me mentally thrive and become more resilient, no matter what the circumstance. Life isn't always so positive, however this discordance can either break us or make us more resilient. When we choose love, this creates more joy, peace, harmony, abundance, and balance, whether our external life situation is up or down.

Listening to my own heart and following my intuition has led me to recreate and reposition my original book 'I am Born Lucky'. The content of these pages forms a powerful manual accessible to everybody.

I believe we are all born lucky. We're all children of love. We all have a unique love to share on this planet. All we need is to choose to live in love, along with a good mindset to positively navigate change and then we can achieve more of what we want in life.

My curiosity and an unwavering belief in love has provided me with a deep connection to my own desires. I have always been intrigued as to why some people struggle or suffer, some thrive whilst others survive. Some people are willing and open, they positively and effortlessly move towards abundance, whilst others see only the glass half empty, why is that? Some are controlled by their fear, pain, or negative conditioning, their lives are lacking yet they seem to feel embarrassed or opposed to seek the path of change, why? We are all unique, yet formed of the same matter, so what separates us from each other and what seamlessly threads us together? Mindset. How we approach life with our minds is how we control the very nature of it.

I cannot create your future for you nor can I tell you how you should manage your emotional and mental wellbeing. But what I can do is teach you the simple ways to help you discover sustainable mental tools to implement positive changes in your life. I can teach you how to connect your whole body to mind and use this to create change. Opening your mind, heart, soul, and spirit every day to allow infinite opportunities will bring you new possibilities and surprises. Together we can form, strengthen, and build an endless stream of love, growth, wellness, and abundance. This could be yours; it is available to everyone.

I would like to thank YOU for the inspiration to write this book and my family, and friends for their loving support. My amazing mummy and my late Pa, who continue to provide me with the eternal sounds of inner belief and love. I LOVE YOU all.

And a massive amount of respect and love to my incredible husband sexy G, and my beautiful sons, Woody and Jasper. You have given me the love, strength, support, and space that I needed to grow, and the confidence and belief I need to move forwards.

LOVE IS A BEAUTIFUL THING.

Let us all awaken our truth and live more in the light of love!

BORN TO LOVE? We are all BORN TO LOVE!

Big Love,

Suzi B xxx

TABLE OF CONTENTS

Introduction 1

Chapter 1: BODY TALK AND THE POWER OF OUR WORDS .. 12

    Dancing with words 14

    Explore the world 17

    Beauty or beast, what do you see? 20

Chapter 2: Connection & Relationships 24

    Connecting confidently 25

    Trust Building 27

    Breathing Love Into Life 31

Chapter 3: Beliefs & Values 33

    Purpose of Life 35

    Inside-Out: The change starts from within. 39

    Calibrate your state 43

    What you believe is what you stand for 43

Chapter 4: Motivation to Change & Cultivating Confidence 47

    Positively focus 49

    Three Types Of Behaviour 49

    Seven Good Habits 51

    Seven Good Habits To Adopt 52

    Get Creative 54

Chapter 5: Fears & Control 57

    Free Fix 59

    Frame your Future 61

    The Mind's Eye 64

C h a p t e r 6: Problem solving made easy 67
    Easy to Change? 69
    Receiving Feedback 70
    Relaxation: Connect With Your Heart 72

C h a p t e r 7: Behaviors & Results 75
    Positive Anchors to stay 77
    The Gift of Time 79
    Making it Happen 82

C h a p t e r 8: Born To Love 85
    Birth Rebirth Delivery 85
    Circle of Trust 87
    Our circle needs to provide 87
    Be the Best You Can Be 89
    Story Time 91

INTRODUCTION

'I believe cultivating wellness within could be the greatest medicine of all, and could heal a nation'

~ Suzi B

We're all unique, linked by simple things that hold us together. Our differences are the threads of the overall fabric that create the beautiful tapestry of life. Our inner purpose, which gives rise to happiness, is the life sower of seeds. These flourish in the fertile ground of realisation that the more you give, the more you receive.

We all have mental health needs and will experience trauma at some level in our lives. Most of us deal with a rainbow of emotions which unravel as we go through life. In today's world, we should prioritise our mental wellbeing and overall wellness. We should learn how to manage our thoughts, feelings and behaviours so we can develop and strengthen ourselves. When we heal, learn, love, connect and receive any kind of positive intervention for our mental health, we are ensuring past events do not negatively affect our own life and future generations.

I am personally grateful for all that I have, for the whole journey, the shame, the pain and the pleasure. I reflect on past generations and recognise what we now know and what we must be grateful for. I feel blessed to be evolving through this lifetime and being given permission to heal and live differently. I also give thanks to the difficult times when life gave me my awakenings. The times when the ground stood still, and my heart expanded widely into the echoes of eternal and unconditional love. Because, it was at these times, I felt most vulnerable. Through the whispers, I could feel love, see the love and be love.

We are not on this journey alone. Every single one of us belongs here. We are all simply making connections, memories and meaning. Being thankful for this knowledge and respecting our own and others' feelings, allows acceptance of ourselves and others. It also frees us from feeling like we are living in the prison of our past and helps us move forward to live in the present moment, to our own our future. This is freedom.

Everything I do is done with love. I know that when we heal our own souls, we also heal those who came before us and those that come after. When we move from struggle and hardship and turn our fears into love, we learn to heal through joy and to truly connect and thrive. The abundance of love and beauty forms a place where we come together and are able to feel deeply loved and present.

I have over 20 years of experience in coaching, mentoring and training, with a passion for mental wellbeing and intuitively empowering and healing those I work with. I share this book with you in hope that one day we all start to prioritise mental wellbeing over what we look like and what material possessions we have. I know that when we create wellness within, this becomes our daily practice, and our standards rise. We shift out of the ego-mind and into the heart. It is only then that life becomes free, innocent and balance is restored. From this place we act from our passion and spirit, so we can freely love, build relationships and get more of what we want in life.

> *'Is the meaning of true love, to love until it hurts?'*
>
> *~ Mother Teresa*

Through the experience of my life and those I work with; I've learnt that most memories we hold are attached to a feeling of pain or pleasure. From a very young age, I chose to love unconditionally through the pain. I'm going to share parts of my experiences with you, in hope that this helps you heal some of your own stories that may be holding you back or preventing you from achieving all that you aspire to be in this lifetime.

When I began to imagine this book, everything else started to effortlessly fall into place. I had this growing idea; I knew I needed to reach more people and felt that no one should be exempt from this learning. I felt a responsibility of putting my knowledge into words and bringing it into the world and giving what I teach, a life of its own. I will prove to you now that no matter what life delivers, we become what we believe and manifest what we project into the world.

I was born a free spirit, someone with folk wisdom and foreknowledge. I inherited an anticipation of the world and life within it, knew what I wanted and held deep morals of respect and value. And not from what others gave to me, but what I gave to myself.

With my bright orange hair and my appetite for life, my journey would not be a dull affair. My childhood and teenage years came with its fair share of dramas. There was confusion, depression, alcohol, bullying, conflict, dishonesty and arguing. We would discuss none of these issues, it was like they did not exist, the book was closed. As a family we did not talk about what was going on, we were just taught to brush ourselves down and get on with it, that is just what we did back then. I remember feeling shame, rejection, a sense of lacking, fear, and hate, throughout those early days. Part of me felt like I was not meant to exist and the other part of me felt like I did not fit in anywhere. The reality is that we have all been hurt at some point in the past, most have experienced anger, pain, frustration, and fear. However, we all have the power to change the energetic charge these feelings have over our mental wellbeing. Once we accept these memories no longer serve us, we can transform our lives for the better. Memories and past events shape our perception of the world as we see it. The decisions we make and how we action these decisions will determine the outcome of an event.

In the midst of my personal memories, I always felt strongly protected and loved. I knew early on that my purpose was to love, share love and be consistently, unapologetically me. Little did I know back then that this confusing start would support my process of discovery. My life within was given substance, and in return it gave me hope and the resilience I needed to pull through. From a very young age, I felt we are all born lucky and we were all born to love.

At the age of 11, my mum married my stepdad and we moved from London to sunny Bognor Regis in West Sussex UK. I loved life and school, however; I found it difficult to learn in a conventional way. At the age of 15, just before sitting GCSE's I was told I was dyslexic. Needless to say, this late diagnosis meant I didn't leave school a grade A student, but this didn't deter me from continuing to share love with everyone around me.

I have always been a social butterfly, I love my friends, love to party, going on adventures, to gigs, festivals and travelling. I love nature, especially the beach and ocean. It helps stay connected to source energy, as does listening to classical music, and meditating with my crystals. Looking back now, I think my connection to universal energy started when my life dynamics drastically changed. Questioning and accepting who I was from such a young age helped me to not only cope but to find my inner courage and strength.

I have always been optimistic. I believe we all have the power to manifest anything we want from life once can fully understand the concept that everything we see came from someone's thought. I have trust that everything happens for a reason, and that right now, we are all exactly where we were meant to be in life. Through this understanding, I have slowly seen myself and my family heal and grow. I know for a child who once felt lonely and unloved, I now feel unconditional love and forgiveness with all my heart. Through this hurt, I connected to my own beautiful meaning of true love.

Using the methods in this book I've gone onto heal and change negative conditionings such as, toxic relationships, anxiety, depression, and other recreational drugs. Of course, my past has impacted my current relationships, because we are consistently being triggered. So rather than seeing the memories as flaws or limitations, I choose to be grateful for how much it has helped me choose how I want to live my life, be with my family and how I want to be as a mum, wife and friend. No one truly wants to live a life of hardship, negativity, fear and have a sad limiting story, do they? We are all destined to grow and move forwards.

I now help people turn fear and trauma in love. I teach people how to rewrite the story and then how to use their story to empower and grow; experiencing the life they truly desire to live, without the pain and sacrifice. I guide them in self-empowerment, balance, wellness within, freedom and to thrive as they create more of what they want in life.

There will always be issues, tension and problems in the family home, and the lesson is this; it's not your job to be controlling of every negative influence that comes into your life. This would be unrealistic.

We all already have the power within to reach our full potential and overcome difficulties, create freedom and live a life we desire. My mission is to empower those I work with, so they truly believe and trust in themselves deeply throughout life. I want them to enjoy the journey of birth, co-creation and have a fulfilling life of forgiveness, love, abundance, beauty, and joy. When you stop surviving you start living and truly thriving.

'Born to LOVE isn't just a word we say, it's an action we take'

~ Suzi B

My first book 'I am Born Lucky' wouldn't have been created if I hadn't had these experiences. 'Born to Love' would not have meaning if I didn't believe we are all born to love and that we are all children of love. This is the feedback loop to wellness and the foundations to the innate magic of life.

We learn that to live in balance; we must fully understand the mind and body connection and how to use this effectively to help us get more of what we want in life and to love without limits. The only happiness in life is to love and to be loved, only love can break your heart, and only love can heal it.

This book is a positive guide to help you manage your emotional and mental wellbeing on a day-to-day basis. This is not so much self-hypnosis as self-management. Over the past twenty-two years, I have practiced Neuro-Linguistic Programming (NLP), a powerful and relatively recent way of making what you want to happen, happen. Self-hypnosis is a component in this. However, it is more about active state management. NLP and the way I use it in this book provides a supportive guide from an encouraging coach, cheerleader and mentor. Helping maneuver you through the transitions of internal to external love.

'Born to Love? Of course, if that's what you want'

~ Suzi B

This book will help enable you to model patterns of quality and study essential forms of behaviour. Sharing this knowledge is not only painless, but it is also positively gratifying. NLP is the technological map of the mind, the science of achievement and the internal neurological curriculum for success. It is being increasingly used in the worlds of business and therapy. Your chiropractor might be a student of it. The person who sells you your car insurance and clothes may well have been trained in it. Programmes on television are informed by it. It is becoming part of the vocabulary of everyday life.

This book uses the techniques of NLP for the purposes that they were profoundly meant for, to create what you want in life, to get what you have strived so hard to achieve. If you let it, Born to Love will make a significant impression on your family and will positively impact your everyday life, your children, community, villages, services, job and your environment. The watchword here is preventive action. This book can be a dynamic force towards empowerment.

The goal of this book is to empower those of you who feel that you are second-in-line in the confidence queue or out of balance and the flow of life and the love you share. Those who are willing to give something new a go, fail and fail again but you keep going to achieve what's important. You can be the Inventor, the Project Manager and the troubleshooter of your life. No one else can live this life for you, save you or change you, unless you yourself believe in the change you wish to become. No one else is at fault, to blame or requires criticism or shame. We are responsible for our own actions, lessons, and imperfect ways. We are all just doing our best with what is available to us at the time. There will be excuses made. Nevertheless, the flower will always need watering. The petals are ready to unfold. No-one should be too busy to replenish the water or arrange the bloom so that everyone can enjoy its beauty. This is our birth right.

They say laughter is the best medicine; I say the best medicine is nature. It flows with the rhythm of the body and draws deeply from the body's natural resources. Nature helps us to manage our wellbeing and mental health from a more holistic perspective. After all, our minds will always need taming and our hearts need nurturing.

With the help of NLP, hypnosis, mindfulness, emotional resilience training and other natural tools, I help people welcome and navigate change, and to understand how their earlier experiences in pre-parturition, babyhood or early life has shaped what they think, and how this exhibits through behaviour, in a positive or negative way.

The tiniest emotions, impulses, and behaviors filter through our genetic map to make us all unique. The shaping process takes over, and we are impacted by the world around us, absorbing information through our pores.

Born to Love is a positive seed for life learning. The teachings of this book are here for the long term. It is not a quick fix or a passing phase, but rather a way of living and learning that will create a natural, complementary style of living, delivering both mind and body outcomes. If you embrace the skills in the pages of this book, you will grow to appreciate the power of your mind and what you, and it, are capable of. It is my pleasure to provide the words to support you in your journey, and to connect with why you were Born to Love and how to positively navigate life with love.

Together we will grow, love Suzi B xxx

'It's easy to change when we know how. Change is a choice, and only a one-second decision away'

~ Suzi B

Becoming SELF AWARE

'Developing our life from unconscious behaviours, habits and standards. To consciously living with self-awareness and maximum choice for optimum health and wellbeing. Reflect on our thinking, then expanding our life, beliefs, feelings so that our actions are aligned, and the love flows freely'

~ Suzi B

CHAPTER 1

BODY TALK AND THE POWER OF OUR WORDS

In this section, we look at simple techniques to enhance your communication and language. The way we communicate is the framework around which most we base other interactions.

The seeds of relationships need to be created and flung into the breeze of our life journey. Some of those seeds will fly around the world. Others will take root and flower in our back gardens. The words we use and who we use them with are crucially important to grow our relationships into those which we enjoy and that benefit us. We create our world with the words we choose to use, our powerful words become our reality.

Some words used in this book may be new to you. If you encounter any new words, why not look them up and discover their meaning? This way, you can grow through knowledge and your experience will flourish. If you are familiar with NLP and other natural development models, commit to sharing your experiences - as in a partnership we can grow to be the best we can be in our search for whole being and contentment.

In this section of the book, I show how to shift your thinking as we change and manage inner beauty. I have found that the quickest way to control and transform our feelings is to first move our bodies. Our feelings, actions and thoughts, act like a feedback loop for wellbeing. Applying this simple method can, in itself, help you live life from the heart, experience more fulfilling relationships and achieve more of what you want in life.

Dancing with words

Words can create bridges or put up barriers. Imagine that you are dancing. Your partner is a natural mover, intuitive, expecting your every move. You slip into each dance step easily and enjoy knowing that he or she is there before you. Language is just like that. It can create bonds, shared experiences, and build lifelong friendships. Or it can put up impassable barriers.

This is a powerful foundation for positive frameworks in all forms of communication, either face to face, online or on the phone. We lead with our words, learn to trust deeply, connect naturally and confidentially and dance freely.

Some simple rules are:

Seeking Rapport.

Knowing what you want in an interaction with someone else is helpful. It will inform the way you communicate, and you are much more likely to see the outcome you are after.

Be Sensitive.

Having a sensory awareness of the impact your communication is having on others is important. The only way that you can know whether you have communicated the message you intended to the other person is by observing the outcome or response.

Flexibility is everything.

Adapt your behaviour until you get the outcome you wish. Observe posture, breathing, skin colour, eye movement, hands and feet gestures, facial expression and changes to the tone and quality of voice.

Outcomes.

Have fun acting on the principle that the meaning of your communication lies in the response that you get, not in what you intended to say.

Your choice of words, how you deliver them, your facial expression and body language all contribute to how they are received by someone. Your face and body language will never lie.

Here are some more tips...

Take the words 'and' and 'but' as an example - 'and it would be interesting to try that new restaurant' or 'but, I don't like Spanish food'

Consider the major difference using words like; might, might not, could, may, may not, could have when compared with words like; must, mustn't, should have, ought to, can't.

Or the words you use when encouraging young people or someone in your team, 'I suspect someone like you can... (pause) ...do that' compared with, 'Get on with it'

Or try asking open questions compared with asking closed questions. 'How would you feel about..?' compared with 'You didn't like that, did you?'

Or how about using open, exploring question such as 'What do you want?' or 'What will that give you?' compared with 'Did you want to do this.' or 'You need to do that'

Which would you respond more positively to? How many people in the teaching or health professions use the latter rather than the former approach?

Here's an exercise to do:

Ask someone a question using open language, facilitating rather than peremptory. Experience how different it feels. Use this approach at home with your family, with clients and colleagues at work. See how people react to you differently.

Practice and apply:

Watch and compare people's learning and reactive styles. Create your own positive, caring relationships with all living things and with man-made items. Make it your aim to understand and to be understood. Take a positive lead in your dance with life.

Explore the world

We use our senses to link our inner world and our outer world. These five senses: Visual (sight), Auditory (hearing), Kinaesthetic (feeling), Gustatory (taste) and Olfactory (smell) are our bridges across which we explore the world. However, it would be impossible to take in everything that is presented to us, therefore we all have our perceptual filters (or representational systems in NLP terms) that filter what we take in and what we leave behind. These filters are individual and based on our own unique experiences, culture, upbringing, beliefs, values and assumptions.

Visual

What we can see, both physically and in our imagination.

Auditory

The sounds we hear externally and in our head are both equally real to us.

Kinaesthetic

This is about feeling externally ('what a rough tabletop') and internally. ('I felt something was wrong')

Olfactory and Gustatory

Sense of smell and taste.

These are linked closely to using our sense of taste and smell to distinguish what we like or trust to pass into our bodies. It is important to remember that other people have very different maps of the world. If you said the word 'beauty' to a group of people, one might see distant mountains, a sunny beach, a lover's face, beautiful music. Whilst someone else may experience an internal feeling.

We use our psychological maps to describe our experiences to ourselves and others. To communicate effectively, we need to connect with and appreciate other people's maps of the world. As human beings, we are showered with thousands of pieces of information every hour of every day. To process this deluge of information we use 'sort filters' rather like a person might use sunglasses to reduce the impact of the sun's rays. These filters are usually what we have grown up using and feel comfortable with, however; it doesn't mean that they are right. These filters process information going in and out of our brains and our hearts, our intuition. Putting our usual filter to one side and selecting a new one can completely change the way we look at the world, creating an entirely new ambience in our life. Using these filters will affect how we view the world and how we are viewed.

Changing filters historically in our memories can also release us from the beliefs we have held for a long time, which may have unconsciously trapped us. A lady that has always believed that she is not good enough or can't love herself unconditionally, may take on a whole new character when she realises that this is just a belief and not a rule.

Here's something to do now:

What beliefs and rules do you hold that do not serve you?

Get a sheet of paper and take some time to write these down and then alongside your answers in another colour write down a more empowering belief you could hold instead. Rules tend to take the form of "If ……,then……..". For example, "If I lose my job then I'm a failure" when you could say "If I lose my job, I'll find a better one"

Beliefs tend to take the form "I am…." or "You are……" or "The world is………..". For example, a negative belief would be "I am a failure if I lose my job" but you could change this to "I am **not** a failure if I lose my job"

Practice and apply:

Observe yourself and others and decide which beliefs and rules are empowering and which ones are limiting. Remember that three repeated actions can trigger a learning process, or if negative, can undo what we have already learnt. In the latter event happening, it can take up to twenty-one attempts to re-establish positive learning. However, the conscious brain can only concentrate on 3 to 4 pieces of information at any one time. Keep things simple and avoid over-complicating your actions.

Things might seem obvious here, however, when put into practice, you could be pleasantly surprised. Most routines, habits and behaviours are established here and momentum grows. Changing our thoughts, what we say to ourselves, our internal chit chatter, can encourage new habits and manners, and in return can help us achieve more of what we want in life.

Beauty or beast, what do you see?

We can't help communicating. As humans, we have a deep need to converse, share and connect. We do this in many ways, verbally, visually and with our bodies. What we do influences people and in return what they do will influence you.

When exchanging words remember the meaning of your communication is the response that you get. The inner meaning will always come through, so be certain that what your body, face or words are communicating is what you want. What resonates with you deeply on the inside is what the mind will seek to achieve and bring to life.

Actions speak louder than words. What your body is communicating is very important. If time is short, body language can say a great deal in a small space of time. It has been established that 60% to 80% of the messages we transmit to other people are through body language and that verbal communication accounts for only 7% to 10%. The rest lies in the tone of voice.

In body language it is important to remember...

These NLP principles could be a foundation to how you communicate through body talk and the words you choose to use:

- You are in charge of your actions and your results
- The person with the most flexible behavior, tends to control the outcome
- We can't help communicating
- Behind every behaviour is a positive intention
- If what you are doing isn't working, then do something else

- There is no failure, only feedback

We unconsciously use body language to communicate, generate positive feedback in our lives and to act towards desired outcomes. This language dominates our actions, but we may not be aware of it. Warm, loving interaction between you and your loved ones not only enhances your relationship, it helps to achieve more of what you want. Your actions will influence people around you and in turn, what they do will influence you. We can not control others behavior, only our own. Through this we can lead positively by example.

Body language underpins all communication. Children respond to this; they will mirror and repeat patterns of observed behavior. Mainly yours! Our partners will be informed by this, and what we manifest in life is projected from this alone. Our body is the vehicle for change and the words we use is the fuel that powers this. How we communicate to ourselves on the inside will be reflected on the outside. This is where our morals and standards are formed and what we expect to attract in life.

Body and facial expressions are a powerful influence. Although a single instance of negative body language is not likely to lead to permanent damage, over time it will have an effect. If you regularly use body language that is open, friendly and respectful, you're likely to display increased confidence and self-esteem for yourself and those around you.

If you discover that you have communicated something other than what you intended, accept this as useful feedback, then be flexible enough to change how you communicate until the response that you want is received.

Here's something to consider now:

Who do you want to be? Beauty or the beast?

Practice and apply:

The words you speak often carry less weight than the non-verbal parts of your communication. It's worth considering the impression you give through your facial expressions and body language.

Stand in front of a mirror, take a moment to look at your face. Talk to your reflection like you are talking to a stranger. How do you appear? Are you frowning, smiling, strained?

Think about your posture when you communicate and compare what feels more comfortable and confident for you. How can communication be more enjoyable and effective?

'We can't always control our thoughts, but we can choose what we focus on'

~ Suzi B

CHAPTER 2

Connection & Relationships

Now we will learn about empathy with others, as this can be crucial if we feel negative about someone we see regularly or think they feel negativity towards us. We look at how we can build bridges as we make room for more purposeful and loving relationships. We find that all good things come to those who seek them; sometimes inner peace and motivation grow from the very moments we question and correct.

Enjoy the sense of being in the moment and being aware of your quest. This self-knowledge is important. The only thing that can stop you from experiencing the beauty and fulfilment of 'now' is a need to be somewhere else.

In this section of the book you will learn more about 'brain breathing' and massage, as well as movement that enhances the awareness of relationships. We look at examples of how you can choose how to breathe and how you can live better. The four methods of breathing - Air, Water, Fire and Earth are essential tools to help manage our mental and emotional needs.

Connecting confidently

Learning more about how we connect to one another can be a rewarding and motivating experience. This exercise will help you discover more about your key relationships, those that are working and those that may need some alterations. I always believe that nothing is forever, and this is also true for all relationships. People come into our lives for a reason. If something isn't working or doesn't feel right, then it most likely isn't meant to be for you at this time.

Imagine now that you're in a team-building exercise and you have to build a pontoon to the opposite side of the river. There is another team on the other side. Traditionally, they will see themselves in competition with you. However, you realise that if you work together, you work better. You begin by throwing a line over. Initially, the other group won't pick it up because they are slightly wary of you. However, one of the more intuitive members of their group eventually grasps it and ties something to it before throwing it back to you. You, in return, tie something bigger and throw it back. In this way, trust builds. Eventually, there is a narrow walkway across the river enabling you to cross. After a while, the two sides are now one and have realised that together they can achieve far more than as individuals. They build the pontoon. It becomes a permanent bridge.

We lock trust in. The weight of the load depends on the level of trust. It takes both sides to build the bridge. If the bridge collapses under the weight of expectation or the burden of distrust, it takes longer to rebuild than to build from scratch. How could you communicate with yourself and others better? How will you maintain that trust in the future?

'Isn't this what we ultimately all want. Though there are some things we can't change, we can change the way we think and feel about it. This is infectious. This is the giving and receiving of life and love'

~Suzi B

Have a go at this:

Think of this reaching out style and write five things which you know will help you build the bridge in your relationships. Are you working together? Getting along? Being honest? Etc. Think of five things which undermine the building of this bridge of trust.

'The foundations of all relationships are honesty, respect and trust. Being consciously aware helps us adapt or change our behavior, thoughts and feelings so you can work together, if that's what we want'

~Suzi B

Practice and apply:

Enjoy your sense of flexibility as you move your mental connection to the dance of life. Use your words to safeguard your new awareness as you think about the inner beauty of what you're achieving. Stop worrying about the challenges of others and focus instead on yourself, as you move out into the limelight to move sinuously with life and love and all relationships.

Trust Building

Who do you need to build trust with?

Are they an equal partner in this process?

Do you have complete trust in yourself and your abilities?

Your ability to communicate trust using positive language, reinforcing communication styles and body language will enable change to take place and your relationships to bond, survive and thrive. This change will take place naturally and subconsciously. You will discover flexibility with your words and gain positive control over your behaviour. Across this bridge you will be able to carry:

- Effective communication
- The motivation of yourself and others
- Positive thinking
- Actions that make a difference
- An understanding of yourself and those around you
- Management of change
- Emotional responsibility

Rather than allow ourselves to be swept along by our emotions, is it possible for us to recognise what our emotions are telling us and adapt our behaviour accordingly to take control? Are we spending too much time in our minds and not enough time listening and responding to the messages of our hearts, intuition, or body? We have to prioritise all our needs for wellbeing to truly flourish.

What is the deeper meaning behind these well lived feelings?

- **Anger:** Act towards what we think is right and accept the things we can't change. What is it that you want and what would be the best way of achieving it?
- **Fear**: Fear is not always bad. It serves to protect us. What is that fear attempting to tell us? How are we going to react to it?
- **Hurt**: This impacts every relationship at some stage, even the most loving, attentive and caring people go through it. We feel hurt if we sense a reduction in our self-worth.
- **Anxiety**: We link anxiety to feelings and creative self-discovery. There are three types of anxiety - a general feeling of worry, a sudden attack of panicky feelings, or a fear of a certain situation or object.
- **Shame**: We feel shame when we think poorly of ourselves or it embarrasses us. This can be a failure to trust our own deepest values. It can be a major motivation for positive change, as it will propel us to go down the route of doing what we want.
- **Frustration:** Is born out of not achieving the results we want. Sometimes it is expressed as a slow-burning form of anger. This can lead to greater clarity over what we want.
- **Guilt**: Is expressed when we feel we are not living true to our principles. However, this guilt may be a reaction to our not fulfilling the standards instilled during our upbringing. Ask yourself each day if you are living to 'your values' or struggling to live up to someone else's. Adjust your behaviour accordingly, to your expectations, dreams and wishes.

- **Sadness:** Bereavement or loss can cause sadness. We care about what we have lost. Sadness reminds us to treasure what we value and to welcome love and caring in the future.

For us to thrive mentally and emotionally, we must build trust in ourselves and reconnect to living from the heart, not just the mind. This can make times of uncertainty feel more solid and in itself can cultivate negative emotions so we can confidently more forward.

'This is a fabulous piece of learning which is simplistically outlined and profoundly effective'
~ Lea Smith

Natural or learnt?

It is your prerogative to change. Your voice can choose to be heard and ONLY you can take action, if that's what you want. Breathing life and love into this knowing can develop faith. There are many ways to breathe, and each of them brings with it its own kind of power. Breathing can demonstrate a relationship with your inner thoughts, feelings and in breathing out forge outward bonds.

Here's something to do now:

Hold the thought in your mind and use the fire or water breathing style to drop down to your core, ground you to feel at home in your heart. How does that feel now?

Air breath – HOLD IN: Breath in for 4 (hold in for 4) Breath out for 4, repeat

Water breath – OUT: Breath in for 4 – Breath out for 8, repeat

Fire breath – IN: Breath in for 6 – breath out for 2, repeat

Earth breath – HOLD OUT: Breath in for 6 – breath out for 6 (hold out for 6), repeat

Practice and apply:

Notice how changing your breathing affects your feelings. Left alone, we naturally breathe like babies do, organically and deep within our bodies. Each emotion has a rhythm of breathing attached to it. You can have full control over both. By accepting this understanding, you can join its flow. Your belief system and higher purpose are there to serve your best interests. They will also serve those of others as we move closer to seek our community of interest together.

Breathing Love into Life

We are all plugged into the mains of the human power grid. We harness, store, and use that power to connect well with others. Our ability to do so is underpinned by our natural inclination (if we allow it) to communicate in ways that the person we are connecting with enjoys. The more we observe, understand and mirror how they communicate, the better we will be at building the bond of trust and of replicating their behaviour, unconsciously they feel that we are on their side. The more we practice this 'mirroring' behaviour, the better we become at it.

At a basic level, this empathy can be incorporated in the rhythm of our breathing and the movement of our hands and feet. It can also be expressed through our clothes, the expressions we wear on our face, the structure and length and speed of our speech patterns and the words that we use. Once we understand that how we present ourselves to others will determine their reaction to us and what we want from them, we can use clothing, hairstyle, sensory preferences, the style of our environment, accessories and even our handwriting (or email style) to build the bridge of communication with those around us.

The difference between matching and mirroring is the difference between copying and complimenting. Don't replicate their every move or expression, simply move and respond in a mirror opposite fashion. They cross their legs to the right; you cross yours to the left. They look out of the window and smile; you look at them and smile. The point is that they do not notice you doing this; it's just that internally they feel comfortable that you are in sync.

Breathing is our connection with life. We breathe to live. To explore the real meaning of that life (and the life we may be carrying) we should endeavour to understand more about the importance of each breath, and how it infuses our life force with purpose and being. When each breath enables us to deeply connect with ourselves and others around us, we will begin to notice that not all types of breathing are the same. It varies depending on the situation and environment.

Here's something to do now:

Think about both the state and the position you would like to be in to benefit your life. What do you need to do to achieve this? How would being calmer and more confident benefit you and your relationships?

Practice and apply:

Think about the style, the tone and rhythm of your voice, body language and breathing when communicating. Explore different emotions, states and positions and apply trust-building and understanding of each other's needs and emotions. Respect every inflow and outflow of your breathing life.

CHAPTER 3

Beliefs & Values

For our root purpose to flower, we need to surround it with the compost of our beliefs and values. The soil in which our ambitions grow is not a constant state, it changes and replenishes over time with experience. Watering this soil is important. If it is constantly renewed, we are likely to feel content and a sense of wellness within. Our past doesn't define our future, we cannot control the future, and attempting to do so would be based on past experiences.

Part of us, of course, will want to undermine this sense of fulfilment, telling us that this oasis of wellbeing cannot be real. However, you might instead choose to think that all is good and that events are working well for and your higher self. After all, your thinking is reality, if you want it to be. Contentment is no one else's prerogative except your own.

Observing how you are working inside, what is working for your greater good, and what isn't, enables you to grow as a person. In this section, we start to look at the roots of change. Roots that can grow and be repositioned, pruned and watered to ensure they create the fruits that represent the person you are, not what other people have labelled you. Planting those roots of belief in the soil of your choice is the difference between servitude and freedom.

The book will help enable you to map across your experiences and point towards more pleasurable and fulfilling moments to share. I will show you how to shift belief patterns and teach you a way to move from old limiting beliefs to ones that will serve you and others for the better. This can be extremely powerful and fast-acting.

> *'Living for today and building on tomorrow. Do you believe in yourself and the life you aspire to live? Are you leading with love and listening to your heart? Are you positively making changes today, that will impact your future wellbeing and all relationships?'*
>
> *~ Suzi B*

Purpose of Life

As we begin to explore the structure of our environment and our purpose within it, perhaps we can take a little time to notice the depth of our life experience and the inner conviction of who we really are.

So, who are you, and what is your mission in life? What are you passionate about? What are your dreams, your visions, your purpose?

A personal mission statement can be a very good idea. It clarifies what you believe, what motivates you and provides direction for the future. Once written down, it doesn't have to be cast in stone. It is your statement of intent, and this will change according to circumstances. However, at the core, it is likely to remain consistent.

Committing thoughts to paper may expose certain beliefs and attitudes that you secretly would like to change. That's fine - it reinforces the need for such an exercise. You will find direction and clarity by searching for these things. In asking 'Who am I?' you begin to take responsibility for the answer. Is someone else really in charge of your life? Are all the actions in your life sympathetic with your aims? Does your behaviour match your inner aspirations? Do you feel blessed to be living your life? If you don't feel this way yet, could you believe that you are abundant and that all events, until now, are preparing you for your future?

As you harness your passion for purpose, love and happiness, it's good to remember that you have a choice of ways in which you decide to give and receive this. Everyone has the power of choice, not just the selected few.

If you want more passion, love and happiness in your life then apply the following steps each day:

- Start your day with the LOVE overload and gratitude list
- Spend 60 minutes a day practicing SELF LOVE
- Remind yourself at least 20 times a day how beautiful you are and promote this love in others
- Sharing makes you happy – share your warmth for others 10 times a day
- Laugh at least 20 times a day
- Smile a minimum of 40 times a day
- Think of 3 or more happy memories each day, remind yourself of the story behind that memory
- Copy the love you have for others and see in others
- Think of 3 or more things that would make you happy in the future
- Make a note of at least 6 things a day that you are grateful for

Monitor each day to see whether you are living according to your values, and if not, take action to move towards them and slowly adjust your behaviour. As with love, the more happiness you give away the more you receive in return. Being happy in yourself is the best preparation for joyful, loving and long-term relationships. The ability to make other people happy is priceless, and the exciting thing is that by doing so, you'll find the shortest route to a happy life. The ONLY happiness in the world is to love and be loved…. Often all it takes is a smile or a kind word. Expressing your primary purpose in life helps to establish solidity, focus, ambition and control.

By expressing some of these innermost desires, we are permitting our unconscious minds to go out and realise them. Our life choices will become affected. We will be far less easily deflected from our goals and more driven towards them. In writing down what our deeper aspirations and beliefs are, we put a destination on our behaviour, like an address on an envelope. We introduce a steely strand of purpose to our life, and the lives of the people we care about. We put ourselves in control. So, if you were placed on this earth to achieve certain things, what would they be? These values inform your purpose in life.

Our values, beliefs and core identity (our purpose in life) can become misaligned or past their sell-by date. If, when you look at your personal mission statement, you discover something that doesn't seem authentic or relevant anymore, note this, and then consider if a more appropriate value could replace it. Speak out loud the values and principles that feel comfortable to you. For example, you may have gained a belief in childhood that states 'I always have to put others first'. You may decide that an alternative such as, 'I will be kind to myself and practice SELF LOVE first, because my health and wellbeing are important to me and my family,' is a more useful belief to go forward with.

Here's something to do now:

What beliefs do you have that you could replace?

Changing beliefs is simple, and so effective. The beliefs you woke up with this morning might not be the same as the beliefs you go to bed with tonight.

Practice and apply:

Remember to ask, 'What else?' and 'What's more important?' Notice the difference when you reach a clear signpost to your desired purpose.

What is the difference between beliefs and values?

Beliefs - your attitude, your viewpoint, an idea or a way of life.

Values - morals, standards, habits, principles or ethics.

Inside-Out: The change starts from within

- 'You shouldn't be doing that, you might fail..'
- 'You should try to please everyone..'
- 'You tried that before and failed, don't try it again..'

Do you recognise these voices? We all have them. They are our neurological early warning system acting to defend us from harm. If we have had a painful or damaging experience earlier in our lives, our brains have learnt that certain experiences can cause us pain and will do its utmost to protect us from anything like that happening again. These critical voices are in fact on our side. However, their good intentions for us have been deflected by our past experience to such a degree that they are now hampering our progress. It is possible to control and reframe these voices. After all, they belong to you.

I believe we all experience trauma at some level in our lives and are dealing with a rainbow of emotions that unravel as we go through life. In today's world, we should prioritise mental wellbeing. We need to learn how to manage these thoughts, feelings and behaviors so we can develop and strengthen all of our wellbeing. When we heal, learn, love, connect and receive an intervention, we are ensuring past events do not negatively affect our own life and future generations. The change starts from within….

Here's an experiment. What is the most common critical comment that plays in your mind? Yes, that one! Now talk to yourself in that critical voice, relaying all the reasons why you shouldn't do something, employing that deeply annoying, critical tone. Hold that thought. Now change the tone of voice, make it someone who cares for you, loves you. What is it saying now?

Did you know that the two sides of our brain provide different functions? However, both sides function for our greater benefit. The different functions all have a positive intention and we can use our minds to scan, accept, reject and install the beliefs and responses that work best for us.

Left Brain Functions – Masculine Energy – Yang Energy

- uses logic
- detail-oriented
- facts rule
- words and language
- present and past
- math's and science
- can comprehend
- knowing
- acknowledges
- order/pattern perception
- knows object name
- reality-based
- forms strategies
- practical
- safe

Right Brain Functions – Feminine Energy – Yin Energy

- uses feeling
- "big picture" oriented
- imagination rules

- symbols and images
- present and future
- philosophy & religion
- can "get it" (i.e. meaning)
- believes
- appreciates
- spatial perception
- knows object function
- fantasy based
- presents possibilities
- impetuous
- risk-taking

Rationalising our thoughts and putting them into perspective can have a massive impact on our relationships and assist us through life, helping us to achieve more of what we want in life. This can help with difficulties and complications. Know that we're not 'failing', we're just learning.

Understanding the purpose of that inner conversation, weighing up the voices for and against, testing the different streams of thinking, will lead you to a place of knowing what you are here for, what decisions to make and what action to take. This ability to rationalise is a symptom of maturity. This function of our brain only fully develops as we enter our teenage years.

Here's something to do now:

Change the tone and the content of that internal critical voice. In doing this, the content of what it is saying is also likely to transform. Eventually, it may grow to sound just like you, with your interests at heart. What would you like it to be saying to you now?

I often observe myself and how other people talk, and question how they hear themselves internally talk?

Practice and apply:

Openly affirming your desired beliefs and actions can reinforce change. Often, when we are outside our comfort zone, we achieve more. Many challenges and obstacles can be better managed from a distance. 'It's not me, it's outside of me, it/she/he has it's/her/his reasons for doing what it/she/he is doing.'

Consciously move that challenge to a place outside yourself, where you can manage it better. Do it now. Move it further away. Does that feel better? Change its colour from colour to mono, shrink it in size, make it laugh, sing, wear silly clothing. It's your choice. Replace the object or person who is causing you this pain with something that you want instead. Does that feel better? Good. Then keep it.

Calibrate your state

What you believe is what you stand for

The ability to control the way you think lies at the heart of fulfilment and a sense of purpose. Your very identity is wrapped up in it. If you have the power to control your personal state, then you have unlocked the key to contentment, success and the realisation of your personal goals. It is like finding the key to the door of your future.

So how do you find this key? Take a moment to read this and then engage with the process below. Take care to observe what is going on inside, as this is the most effective way of managing deeper self-change.

Create some space, close your eyes and focus your attention inside yourself. Notice the level of self-conversation inside you at this moment, that voice inside that comments on your thoughts, action and emotions. Is it loud or soft? What tone are you using to speak to yourself? Do you sound gentle or harsh, authoritative or friendly, urgent or relaxed? Do the words support and encourage, or is the voice critical? Just listen.

Now notice your emotional state. What emotion is present? Are you excited, nervous, angry, happy or something else? Finally, monitor your body, how does it feel? Energised, tired, hurting, do you feel anxious anywhere? What else?

Now open your eyes… Listening to an internal self-conversation is a useful habit to adopt as it enables you to monitor the changes you are making on the inside. You may have already noticed a change, as just being aware of your inner state can create shifts in your outward behaviour and your inner feelings.

Taking control of your mind is something that you can choose to do. Having done it, you may find that you inevitably take control of other parts of your life. Your memories and life experience belong to you. If they are not serving you well, then it is your right to change them.

Learn how to recognise and press those buttons, use a different voice, allow yourself to say friendly, kind, supportive things to yourself. If you can do it for you, you will learn how to do it for others too. In the process, you will create an environment around you, a protective shell that enables you to operate at maximum capacity for you and the people closest to you. Remember that your behaviour is not your personality; it is something that you do. And you can change it.

Believing in something presupposes a commitment to it. Agreeing or disagreeing with an idea usually shows that we have a belief about it. The idea is not the belief:

- Beliefs are ideas you have a commitment to and support.
- They are the views and opinions that represent you.
- Your beliefs are positions that you endorse, consistently.
- Beliefs express your attitude and outlook.

Ask yourself these questions;

> Q: What behaviours and attitudes have you absorbed from others?
>
> Q: When did this happen?
>
> Q: Are they doing what you want them to?
>
> Q: Whose beliefs have you inherited?
>
> Q: How has this shaped your life to date?

This exercise is simple and easy to follow and is great to take into all areas of day to day life.

Now try this;

What have you already decided to change? Who else does this affect?

Practice and apply:

Describing your deepest aims and desires can be done without words. Our outer actions and body language may well do the job better. However, knowing what you want to change is central to this process. Once decided, the change has already begun. Be alert to what is constantly jockeying to claim your attention, what would you like to focus on instead? Notice who is in control. You can decide to change, and that decision will change others too. What would you like to change? How will that impact others?

'Everything is achieved through forgiveness love and kindness'

~ Suzi B

CHAPTER 4

Motivation to Change & Cultivating Confidence

This is the point of traction, the point at which the rubber hits the road. It's where a desire to change takes shape and starts moving.

Motivation aided by confidence will take you where you want to go. It is the fuel for the engine of your life. With it, you can lead by example, learn by your mistakes and shake off the false garments of someone else's energy. This part of the book is for the brave of hearted, those who dare to change.

Understanding the power of change is like installing satellite navigation for where you are going in life. It also acts as a magnet for others. Notice what you admire in others and adopt it. Encourage and motivate others as you consciously move in the new direction that you have chosen.

Share this moment fully with life and all your relationships. You will travel faster and further together. The language you use on this journey will be like the wind. If used wisely, it will blow kindly on all concerned.

Positively focus

Once we are able to form our thinking, plan our actions and move decisively towards our goals, we are taking crucial steps towards realising our dreams. At the root of this process is belief. To know what we want, to understand that it is more important to move towards something than away from it. If we are clear in our mind what we want to achieve, this knowledge or belief will lead to solutions finding themselves.

We base progress on belief. If you believe you can, then you can, and if you believe you can't, you are probably right. Behind every behaviour is a positive intention. Attitudes and behaviour underpin the way we think, feel, act and how we react to the world around us. They determine the quality and effectiveness of our thinking and the positive or negative consequences of our behaviour. We base our attitude upon our expectations and perceptions - our definition of reality.

Three Types of Behaviour

Where do you see yourself here?

1. Maybe - Spectators with Neutral Attitudes

Spectators watch life happen and observe others. They play it safe and work hard to avoid risks. Spectators are afraid of change. They often are tired or detached. Their defining word is: 'Maybe'. Their most popular action: coasting. Typical phrases: 'I doubt it', 'I might', 'I don't know' and 'I'm hesitant'.

2. No - Critics with Negative Attitudes

Critics look at life and complain. They criticise after the fact, imposing their 'expertise' and find fault in others. Critics dislike change. They often appear frustrated or pessimistic. Their defining word is: 'No!' Their prevailing action: Stop! Typical phrases: 'I can't', 'I won't', 'No way' and 'You made me'.

3. Yes - Players with positive attitudes

Players actively participate in life and embrace opportunities. They take risks and are willing to make mistakes. Players enjoy learning and change. They are usually confident and optimistic. Their defining word is: 'Yes!' Their prevailing action: Go! Typical phrases: 'I can', 'I will', 'I'm sure' and 'I choose to'.

Instead of being critical of new ideas, why not look for new opportunities and wait to be affirmed, or otherwise? Be alert to new possibilities. We could face change positively and learn how best to go further in your search for what you want in life. In this way, you will notice what's important as you open options and take positive control of your mind, body and spirit.

Here's something to do now:

What steps are you currently taking? What would it be like to believe you really can be, do and have all that you desire?

Practice and apply:

Your brain is set up to work hard on your behalf. It has your best interests at heart. It will act with you to achieve all those things you have ached for if you let it. It is important to focus on what you want, not the negative things that you may have heard or picked up along the way. Ask what you want. What are you prepared to do to get it?

Consider this. Could the very thing that is stopping you, be a shortcut to achieving it? What would happen if you faced it and went beyond it to what you desire on the other side?

Seven Good Habits

Our character or personality is merely a collection of our behaviors that enable others to recognise us. Our behaviour is motivated by knowledge, skill and desire. Knowledge allows us to know what to do, skill gives us the ability to do it, and desire is the motivation behind it. We acquire these as we move through life. Self-control is the knowledge that we have these things, and that they are under our direction. The seven habits overleaf will enable us to control this process and move us through the three stages of our life, which are:

1. Dependence: our state when we are born and in infancy, relying on others to take care of us.
2. Independence: when we make our own decisions and take care of ourselves.
3. Inter-dependence: when we realise that if we cooperate, we may achieve something that cannot be achieved independently.

Seven Good Habits to Adopt

1. Be proactive

Change starts from within. Effective people decide to improve their lives through the things that they can influence rather than by passively reacting to outside forces.

2. Begin with the end in mind

Extend the mission statement into long-term goals based on personal values.

3. Put first things first

Identify the key roles that you have in life and make time for each of them.

4. Think win-win and win

Seek agreements and relationships that are mutually beneficial, then find the third win beyond these.

5. Seek first to understand, then to be understood

Effective listening is not just echoing what the other person has said through the lens of one's own experience. Rather, it is putting oneself in the other's perspective, listening empathically for both feeling and meaning.

6. Synergise – seek allies

Through mutual trust and understanding, it is often possible to solve conflicts better in partnership than alone.

7. Sharpen your senses

Maintain the balance between the physical, mental, social, emotional and spiritual spheres. Have the confidence to move between them and avoid spending too long in just one.

Here's something to do now:

Think about the love you share and the life you aspire to live. How would applying these seven principles to the way in which you relate to life make a difference to you and to others?

Practice and apply:

Why not make every moment magical? Use the seven principles to do this, learn, grow and support the process of change in each other. Make the most of everything you encounter to find understanding in it and those around you.

Listen to the music of your life. Enjoy the sensation of the moment and look at how your dance is changing as you listen and grow. Are you dancing with someone or apart? How could you be more creative by dancing in a partnership? How much more could be achieved in the community than alone?

'Trust in yourself and co-create beautiful things'

~ Suzi B

Get Creative

It's good to visualise your destination. Your mind and body need some kind of direction, they're not interested in the 'how' they just need to know the why. This helps us to move towards the things we want and not towards the things we don't want in our life.

The journey between your present state and your desired state is the process of change. Obstacles are the difference between the two. We often see issues in our life as problems. This might be why we get stuck, if we call obstacles or challenges 'problems' then we will see them as difficult to overcome and this process may become a 'problem'.

Change (in thinking and circumstances) may well be the simplest key to progress. Consider these questions:

- How many times have you laboured over a problem and not seemed to have got anywhere?
- How many times has a solution appeared when you have not been focused on the problem?

Would it be useful to have a new way to approach problems? If we're not careful, describing difficult stages in our development as 'problems' can become a habit.

What we have discussed is a useful way of shifting from problem thinking to outcome thinking. When issues are approached in this way, creative solutions appear. We use a different way of thinking when we focus on the result rather than the problem.

Here's something to do now:

In your mind, take yourself to the outcome you want to achieve, then think about what it would be like when you arrive there? What you will hear, see and feel on arrival? Bring this sensation back into your heart. This will enable you to find new ways of getting there.

Practice and apply:

The anticipation of opportunities and their creation will both forge a path to your dream. Decide whether you are master of your destiny or whether you are being driven by forces outside yourself. Can you change these forces?

Apply this criterion to as many situations in your life as possible. Check that your beliefs and values are supporting you and those you share life with. When you are satisfied that they are, share with the people you care about and let them know that they can change the soil in which their life is rooted in and can plant their own ambitions, rather than accepting the cuttings and weeds of others. It's like the traffic lights in your life all turning green at once!

'It's not about how much you do, but how much love you put into what you do that counts.'

~ Mother Teresa.

CHAPTER 5

Fears & Control

Our fears often point to places we need to go. Feeling stuck can lead directly to a secondary gain when we overcome our inner, sometimes imaginary obstacles. Often, times like these can be positive as we discover what we are capable of. However, there is a danger of getting stuck if we believe that we can't overcome it. When we breathe life knowledge into this area, we will see dramatic change and will be able to communicate what we want confidently to ourselves and others.

This book takes you through an easy to adopt a solution that enables you to reframe your future and kick-start your future intentions. Allow fear to be heard, however not be in control.

Free Fix

Human beings are naturally curious. We seek to make meaning of the world around us and when we don't have access to clear meaning about a particular situation, we will make up our own. Once this has happened, it becomes part of the fabric of our experience and as we grow, we learn to trust our judgement. However, this can become an obstructive certainty that we are always right in our judgement. At this point, our brain stops questioning attitudes and behaviors that ordinarily it would challenge.

Before the age of ten, we have often made most of the major decisions and value judgements on which we base our life from that point. However, although our thinking might be shaped by this point, it is not too late to change it.

We often describe extreme behaviour caused by previous experience as a phobia. Trauma fixes in us a rigid and often difficult to manage response to everyday situations. Trauma can instill in us attitudes and automatic responses that might have taken a split second to create. In one sense, trauma is speed learning. We can learn phobias in a second that can last a lifetime, particularly if more than one sense formed part of this experience.

Post-Traumatic Stress Syndrome, for example:

- **Kinaesthetic:** Pain either visual or physical witnessed in an accident or incident.
- **Visual**: Seeing pain and distress
- **Auditory**: The loud sound associated with the incident
- **Olfactory:** The smell of blood or spilt oil

From that point, everything associated with that incident will be converted into a loudhailer shouting 'Stay Clear!' Usually, we can point to the moment when the phobia formed, unless our mind has suppressed this emotion, then we may not be able to identify how we came to be afraid of spiders (for example) until we return to the starting point and re-frame the memory of it. In other words, fears are usually learnt behaviors - and this process can begin in the womb. This can also be part of a past generational pattern or event past life events, if you believe in that!?

Our mind is over 2 million years old and its primary instinct is survival, fear, pain and pleasure. Fundamentally they all love who we are and have our best interest at heart. The mind needs to be heard, although it doesn't need to lead the way...

As adults, we can often instill many limiting beliefs and unwanted values in our lives and in the lives of those around us. This can slow the ability to make changes quickly in later life. The good news is that it is possible to change minds and free emotions to gain results quickly and simply. And you can do this yourself. Because we can learn a fear or phobia in an instant, we can unlearn it in almost as short a time. Fear is good. It serves to protect us. Understanding that all of our fears are working (perhaps mistakenly) for our good is the first step towards managing and changing them.

Here's something to do now:

Think about how your fears might prevent you from making the most of the world? Fear and excitement have the same chemical composition inside your body. What would happen if you called that fear excitement instead? What would happen if you called it LOVE instead?

Practice and apply:

The power of our imagination can sometimes become overwhelming and as a result, creates moments that we may want to change or perform differently. The primary action is to know when this has happened. The second step is to evaluate what you want to change and then, third, change from the inside to gain the outcome you want. This works with everything, from the smell of a cabbage boiling to the taste of fear at the prospect of a visit to the dentist.

TURN FEAR INTO LOVE and BREATHE.

Frame your Future

Design your Future

Your perception of time is an experience unique to you. The brain interprets time in a very elastic way, which is why you can often remember events years ago better than you can remember yesterday. Time can sometimes seem slow and at other times fast. Your brain will position its memories of the past and its memories of the future along a continuous 'timeline'.

As we discovered in the section about phobia, our brains will protect us by dealing with how we process events from our past, perhaps by removing the memory altogether, taking us out of the memory or by shortening it changing the timeline.

We all have time preferences. Some people prefer to be 'in time' where they experience everything immediately in the present and have very little perspective on situations. Others will be 'outside time' and prefer a more considered, objective view of time, such as keeping a diary, planning ahead and not reacting emotionally to events around them. Children are usually 'in time'. Reacting immediately and passionately to events. Some adults almost seem disconnected with events and become time observers.

If we stand on the timeline of our life, then events a long way away in terms of years will be more distant behind or in front of us. The timeline itself may be short or long. It may start behind you, run through you and disappear into the future; or it may be short, or stretch like an arc in front of you where you sit as an observer looking at it from outside time. All these positions have meaning and can be changed to suit your needs. Someone who sees themselves out of time can, for example, choose to be inside time and may develop better relationships with people and events because of it.

Grounding exercise or daily self-love practice can help us to connect better to our own timelines and this can assist us to achieve more of what we want in life.

Making it work for you:

The timeline can work for you and help you achieve more love, fulling relationships and achieve more of what you want in life.

Unreel your timeline and place it on the floor, use any kind of rope or string to represent your timeline. Stand on the place that represents today and look towards the future. Then leave the line and walk to and stand at the place you are looking at and reflect on what you did to get there. Enjoy the sensation of having achieved that thing you wanted and now value. Notice all the things you did between the present and where you are now standing. What did you discover about yourself in doing this?

Here's something to do now:

Choose a point in your future where you feel that you will know more than you do now. What is it that you have learnt? What would happen if you applied it now? How would it affect the future of you, your loved ones and your family?

Practice and apply:

I'm a massive fan of vision boards and positive intention setting.

A friend of mine wanted a particular car. So he put a picture of it on his wall. Every time he looked at it he felt more motivated to move towards achieving it. Eventually, he owned that car. Having a picture of what you want on the wall, on your desk, or simply in your mind will encourage your journey towards it.

Sometimes the physical awareness of the things we want to move away from will have a similar impetus on us. The most powerful method is to visualise yourself doing something that you want. Pictures, mental images and physical reminders will all encourage you as you move towards your destination.

The Mind's Eye

Map of Reality and Perception

Everyone has their own version of reality. Two people sitting next to each other in the same room may be seeing completely different things. One may observe the view out of the window. The other may listen to the radio and dream of their summer holiday. Our perception of reality comes from the inside. What we see as objective reality may well be our own personal reality which differs from that of other people.

- People respond to their map of reality, not to others reality
- We make sense of the world through our senses and from our personal experience; this means that each individual's perception is different.
- In communicating effectively, we need to understand and appreciate other people's maps of the world.
- We have to show compassion towards ourselves and others

Part of your mind will have a map of the world and you will acutely know of the environment that you wish to inherit and live in for future generations. You might feel an understandable concern about the effects of the economy and how you choose to live and support the growth and life of the environment we share today.

Our spatial memory defines the mental map we use to plot and call up recollections of the past and what we have already thought about our desired future. It's the storage facility that we've used to collect our past and future memories until now. Consciously changing their position on the map will alter, perhaps fundamentally, how we remember and experience them. The map is your property. What you add to it and signpost on it is up to you. How exciting is this?

Here's something to do now:

Look at your map. How is it being drawn over the next few years? What would you like to add to it? Is there an arterial route on it, or a series of crossroads and side turns?

Practice and apply:

What are your priorities? Who are your partners? Share them and enjoy each other's stories of what is important to move incoordination, and with your own styles. Your home will benefit as change becomes easier to accommodate with a higher level of understanding and a shared pursuit of freedom.

Retain in the front of your mind the principles you believe in. Emulate the actions and life maps of those that you strive towards. If you know what you believe, others will too. Decide what you want and act towards it. Adjust if you have to and always keep the end in mind.

'Life is made up of thoughts, feelings, beliefs, choices, decisions, and actions. Our experience creates the difference and we see what we focus on'

~ *Suzi B*

CHAPTER 6

Problem solving made easy

Do you pass the parcel or prefer to unwrap the problem? We all have a unique perspective of what the perfect gift looks like. A vision that we alone can create. In this section, we look at the process of change and how we can influence others.

Freedom begins in this part of the discovery process. Exciting, isn't it? Finding out what works best for you is top of the agenda. There are many alternatives and you will have fun exploring them.

The watchword here are 'blame or fault'. These two words enable us to pass the responsibility from ourselves to others and in the process, we start to work to others' priorities, not our own. We can, however, use this experience as an invaluable learning process and instead of receiving criticism we can enjoy receiving feedback from others and use it to grow.

This book will enable you to manage the process of change as you learn to detach and reattach yourself to situations and the goals you decide to pursue. I also show how you can use your relationship with your surroundings to ground yourself and positively address problems.

Easy to Change?

Procrastination: putting off until tomorrow what we should do today is a modern disease. Most of us have a clear purpose; yet seem to be able to invent almost limitless ways of avoiding achieving this.

However, having a firm and focused idea of what you want is a very good beginning. Defining the outcome you want convinces your brain to move in a direction towards it. You will move towards your goal, even when you are asleep. Whatever area of your wellbeing you are focusing on, wherever you choose to breathe, love or which relationships you wish to improve. This will become a well-defined outcome, with measurable aims and perfectly realisable goals. It will motivate you, not frighten you.

If you believe you may fail, you are much more likely to. The brain concentrates on the biggest thing in front of it. You may be in danger of creating the very outcome you least want by concentrating on it. Setting up defences to protect you from the worst that could happen is missing the point as those defences may protect you from all kinds of experiences that you would like to experience along the way. Confronting our fears and turning them into gateways is a way of taking back control over our lives. We name the fear, confront it and move beyond it to the place that fear was protecting us from.

Successful goal achievers set their objectives, and instead of asking why they can't achieve them, ask how they can. If you have hit a barrier in setting your outcome, or have a separate issue that seems overwhelming, instead of defining it as a problem, why not see it as a door that when unlocked, will lead directly to your destination?

Here's something to do now:

Decide what you want. Act positively towards it. Then see what happens and adjust accordingly. What would you like to change? Is what is stopping you merely a belief? What would happen if you changed that belief for a better one?

Practice and apply:

Here's a commitment for you. Each event, random or not, can be an opportunity for you to move into new territory and claim it, for you and your family. Taking responsibility for your life and understanding where the opportunities lie even in adversity is the key to achieving your goals. How you do this will also inspire others and provide an example for future generations to follow.

Can you see the positive side to things first now or do you still consider the pitfalls? Take the opportunities as they arise.

Receiving Feedback

It's natural to think about the future, what we might contribute to it and what our gift to the next generation might be. If your friend had a gift that would tangibly improve your life and that could make you a better person, parent, family member or leader, would you ask for it? Of course, you would. If it was a gift that kept on giving, how much would that be? If I gave you a fish, you would not go hungry today, but if I taught you how to fish, you will never go hungry again. The gift is feedback and most of us don't ask for it or know how to accept it. We tend to resist criticism and disagree with people's opinions if they differ from our own. Why is this?

Disagreeing is a very basic form of defence. However, deciding to positively receive this gift of feedback will open the door of change, open up relationships and enrich communication and understanding. After all, what's worse: being criticised or being ignored? Positive feedback means that someone cares enough to tell you. Remaining silent about your shortcomings could be interpreted as seeing you as someone not worthy of attention.

The trick when offering feedback is to sandwich your recommendation for a change in between two slices of encouragement and praise. That way, there is no failure, only feedback. If what you are doing isn't working, do something else. Exploring ways of enabling people to become better must be preferable to looking for problems to chip away at. Creation is always more satisfying than destruction. More can be achieved together, than alone.

Here's something to do now:

Who would benefit from some loving, constructive feedback from you? What might you learn from a good friend who gave you some feedback?

Can you apply this method to yourself, when you give praise or review criticism for change?

Practice and apply:

Make sure there is room in your life for unexpected wins. Each new day offers fresh opportunities. Dolphins come out to play, sing and swim each day. If they worried about the state of the environment or the dangers of being mistaken for sharks, they wouldn't.

Seek to engage with others, learn from these encounters and apply this learning to change. Your clarity of purpose and acceptance of positive feedback will lead to progress, LOVE and happiness. Don't react defensively, just absorb. You will grow as a result.

'Choose love and achieve more of what you want, YOU decide'

~ *SuziB*

Relaxation: Connect with Your Heart

It's not what we're doing, it's how we're choosing to live and spend our time here that truly matters.

Relaxation is not a cure. Relaxation is how you will encounter the insights and illumination into what you want. We can achieve relaxation in a myriad of different ways, via meditation, self-love practice, exercise, sleeping, crystal healing or pampering whichever method you choose. It will enable you to open up your mind to experience the moment. Released from the chit chatter of everyday concerns, your mind will open like a sponge to receive the pure energy of light, love and the world around you.

A minute a day can make a difference. Give it a go and you'll see; this is the only way to truly connect to our hearts desires and make more love in this world.

- What would it be like to be carefree in your daily life without being careless?
- Wouldn't it be good to flow from moment to moment without being stressed and bound in thought?
- Wouldn't it be nice to gracefully create movement in your life without freezing with fear?

To relax is an art in itself and the more you appreciate every moment, the more moments you will have to appreciate. Welcoming your higher self to those moments when you can truly meditate, ponder, explore and play will unlock creativity, passion, love and abundance is all areas of life and wellbeing.

Relaxation is a resource you can dip into at any time, not just at private moments. First, position how you want to feel at the core of your being, and then mirror that sensation on the outside. Take stock of how this feels and project forward to how you will feel when you have succeeded. Do this in a friendly, loving and compassionate way. Being kind to yourself will give birth to lots of other pleasant surprises, this is the center of the feedback loop for wellness within.

Involve everyone in this relaxation experience. They will enjoy having it at the core of their lives. All your emotions can be nurtured, cared for and turned into positive experiences if you treat them like your children. We can achieve this state of fluidity and spontaneity in a matter of seconds, yet results can last for decades… Becoming the change you want to see in this world, naturally happens when you connect to your heart. Once connected, the flow is infectious and everlasting.

'Learning about breathing and taking a moment to find that calm place can help you to manage your emotions and be there for yourself and loved ones. Raise your standards, change your habits and routines, will create inner strength to thrive through the more challenging moments'

~ Kate

You can connect more deeply to your heart now – simply apply this.

1. Relax

Take a deep breath, roll the neck a few times and shake out any knots or kinks.

2. Open Up

Open up your body to the world. Keep the head and chin up, keep your arms open, shoulders back and chest expanded. This communicates confidence in your ability to let other people into your world.

3. Smile

A smile is a universal welcoming gesture of good feeling. Breathe LOVE, IN and OUT

Here's something to do now:

What would it be like to relax when and where you wanted? Just do it and see what happens.

Practice and apply:

If you manage your behaviour with your goals in view, then amazing things can happen. Enjoy new things without being afraid of the consequences. Encourage others to do the same. Notice in this process where deep relaxation is to be found and get more. Compare this with what you usually do. If it is better, make the changes necessary to allow you to do more. With this new inner balance, enjoy your freedom and teach others to share it with you.

CHAPTER 7

Behaviours & Results

Whilst time marches forward, we inhabit the moment and our actions help form that moment and the moments to come.

In this section, we explore the significance of the gift of time. Both our positive and negative behaviours are likely to have been learnt, both can have a positive intention. It is useful to understand how time and space interact to create situations that work for your benefit, before carefully storing how it happened so you can reproduce it when required. In this way, you can create your own collection of magical moments which can be called up whenever you want them. If you find yourself stuck, use other sections in this book to free your outward communication until the desired outcomes arrive. The idea here is to create more time out, to understand differences in time.

As you do this, you will find that you are increasingly leading by example, and as your clarity and sense of purpose grows, you will increasingly be able to appreciate other people's maps of the world.

Take stock of your life in the snapshot of now. This is a powerful exercise which is connected to the very basis of your actions, linking the past with positive pictures of the future will enable you to take active steps towards the future that you want.

Positive Anchors to Stay

The ability to create a state of wellbeing, harmony and creativity will be a huge asset to you. There are anchors in our life that enable us to create and recreate these. Every experience we have had has a sensory reference; visual, auditory, touch, smell and taste. Any one of these elements will bring back the whole of the experience for you to draw upon.

It is an excellent idea to find out what your anchors are. Some will be useful resources, walking through your front door, being hugged by your children or friend, looking at a picture of yourself when you were a child, etc. Some will put you into an unhelpful state – meeting a certain person, going into a particular office, hearing a unique phrase. Once you have identified these, you can decide on your response. You are back in control.

You can also use anchors for a particular resource state so you can access it whenever you need it. Simply decide what state you want - confidence, calmness, relaxation - and then remember a time when you had that state. Impersonation is another way of attaining this state. Think of a person who has achieved what you want to achieve. How would they behave in this situation? What characteristics did they exhibit that you would like to have at your disposal? Patterns of behaviour are often called routines. We can use them as anchors in our life to help us connect with who we are and what we want in life.

Here's something to do now:

Imagine getting up in the middle of the night and not being able to get back to sleep. What state would be most useful to you in doing this? Think of someone who would cope admirably in that situation. How could that person be you?

Practice and apply:

Why not find someone who has something that you want and emulate them? Alternatively, think of someone who you don't admire and seek to be different. Make sure that the way you behave is true to your beliefs, values, aims and purpose. To start with, conjure up the things that form the essential anchors in your life. It could be how good that first drink tastes in the morning, a walk on the beach, a song on the radio. Then consider how you can further improve your environment, your life and your family. It could be through music, your story time, calm time, playtime, recovery time, or through better hygiene. Not only will you bring back to mind the good times, but you will also help create the memories of the future.

Anchors can be so powerful in helping us to manage our emotions and wellbeing. Simply anchor onto something which you want and the use it when you need it.

The Gift of Time

Time started before you were born and will go on after you die. It is in abundant supply, yet, there never seems to be enough of it. A gift of time can be one of the most valuable gifts anyone can share; time that can brighten up one's life, even for a brief moment. It leaves memories that will last till the next time. Time is precious and you will find your own natural method of time processing.

Time processing is how we record and store experiences over time. It gives us a sense of perspective; it tells us whether something happened five minutes or five years ago. It allows healing and when we remember our mistakes, it protects us. We are free to create 'future memories'. You can create these fully equipped with pictures, sounds and feelings, and even smell and taste.

By moving forward on your timeline and 'remembering' these events, it allows your mind to see how you fulfilled your life aims and see ways of achieving these that you might otherwise not think of. The anchors you create to take you back to a place which was supportive and energising for you can also be summoned up quickly, even though the physical event was long ago. Sometimes we would like to forget what we have experienced – or go back and replay it in a way that we would prefer. However, the learning that we take from that time of experience is likely to be priceless. Isn't that worth celebrating?

Time is a gift that enables us to review our lives and make changes to enable us to become better human beings. Time allows us to seek forgiveness for wrongs we've caused, to forgive, to alter our perception of others, to adjust how we view ourselves, to add value and build our self-worth and ultimately to improve the world around us.

Some different aspects of time:

- Important Time
- Interrupted Time
- Escape Time
- Relaxing Time
- Dream Time
- Play Time
- Action Time
- Self-Love Time
- Bed Time

The minutes and seconds within these periods are identical, yet somehow, the way that time moves in each of these is quite different. Remember that time waits for no one.

This can help you put life into perspective and begin to make daily changes to help you live for the day. We can enjoy making more memories together and take full advantage of the moments you share.

Yesterday is history. Tomorrow is a mystery. Today is a gift. That's why it's called the present!

From the point of your birth (and before that) you have been accumulating moments in time that contribute to the person you are. Those experiences are yours to do what you like with. You can learn from them, store them for future reference, ignore them or erase them completely. As you find your place in time and start working with it as a resource, you will become adept at managing it and discovering how to move between in time and out of time.

Here's something to do now:

Stand on your own timeline. Go to the point on it where you're twenty years in the future. What did you decide to do that made an essential difference to your life and development twenty years from now?

Practice and apply:

As we live our lives, time continues on its everlasting journey. Understand your role in time and how you can use time to achieve your purpose. Befriend it, enjoy it, explore it and ultimately, accept it. Time will then become your ally, not your enemy. If you want to, use time to heal the bad moments and grow the good ones.

Making it Happen

As part of this journey to inner knowledge and relaxation, ensure that you fully experience what is happening in the present moment. Notice and take in every little detail, see, smell and taste it. This is the active part of the discovery process and your clarity of direction, a full appreciation of everything your senses are telling you and a curiosity about what could happen next will help you as you step into your exciting future.

Anticipate how you will react to the additional pressures in your life and see how you coped with those demands. Look at the strategies you used to remain calm, confident and in control. Store those anchors for when you will need them. Keep those borrowed behaviour patterns in a safe place. They are yours to use and support yourself with.

The more emphatically you define what you want, the more likely you are to achieve it. As conscious, self-directed adults, we have the power to make things happen. How exciting is that? This is about being mentally and emotionally prepared for your future. You can begin to gather the resources you need to achieve your dreams.

Some of these resources will be internal, some external. Put them in your seed barn for when you will need them in the future. Focus emotionally on things you want. Your mind and body will do the rest.

Sit down and do a life audit. Are your current values, beliefs and the people you share them with compatible with the rest of your experiences hopes and aspirations?

Here's something to do now:

Are you already the person you want to spend the rest of your life with? If not, what needs to change? What are you going to do about that? Remember: dream, believe, achieve.

Ask yourself the following:

- What is your purpose? You decide.
- What is your mission? Is it to be abundant in all areas of your life and wellbeing? What else?
- What are your beliefs and values? What motivates you? What do you believe about your future? What about those in your life? What do you believe about their role?
- What do your capabilities enable you to implement in terms of plans and strategies?
- Which specific behaviours do you have that support you and which that do not?
- What about your environment? Where are your external constraints and opportunities? What are they?

What would the very best version of you do at this moment and how will you make this happen?

Practice and apply:

Monitor your journey as often as you can. Use the earlier sections to enable you to do it. It will give you clarity and purpose as you and your family grow together. Celebrate the things you share, recognise your differences and resolve to make the changes. Notice these things as you move towards a deeper understanding of each other's dance of life. Keep testing the results and changing accordingly, in line with your dreams and aspirations.

CHAPTER 8

Born To LOVE

Delivery, Birth, Rebirth

It is your right to decide how you live your life. You are the author, the producer, the implementer and the creator. It is your time.

In this section, we explore the true meaning of being BORN to LOVE, delivery, birth and rebirth. This is not something that is confined to your own birthing stories; it rolls out into your circle of life. Its energy is everlasting and changing, so if what you are doing now isn't working, it is your right to do something else.

It is good to understand a deep knowledge of yourself and what is right for you. This knowledge can adapt and evolve so that each moment you experience has its own magic and behaviour. Both within ourselves and with each other, we can grow and learn to achieve so much more.

Through this book I will help to bring your circle of life into being. To support and envelop you, both in this moment and in all the moments to come. Step in and out of the circle. See what happens when you do. The breadth of resources at your disposal may surprise you. Christen this space, your circle of life. Call it your kingdom. It belongs to you and it will sustain you.

Circle of Trust

Natural and optimum health is our right. Science today has become part of our circle of trust and we welcome this. However, it doesn't mean that we can't add into this modern process some simple, natural resources that we can bring in ourselves and which will underpin our sense of achievement. There is no right or wrong approach, merely what is right for us. Our body will discover the resources it needs to heal and evolve, either way.

Life is a consent flow of ups and downs. When we create a good solid foundation in a circle we trust, magical things happen.

Our circle needs to provide

- Love
- Respect
- Protection
- Trust
- Support

To feel and appreciate this on the outside, we must first own it on the inside. Do the work it takes to fully connect to these values. Develop skills, tools, freedom, clarity and confidence to mentally and emotionally thrive. Because when we struggle, contract, live from a place of pain and feeling of lacking in life, life becomes difficult. Everything else seems hard and nothing seems to flow, work or go to plan. We should not feel overwhelmed or feel like we're failing when we ask for help and support, prioritise our mental health and wellbeing or want to improve ourselves on a deeper level.

Things in our life have to die for us to birth new things, explore new rebirths and deliver our true purpose in this lifetime. This is another feedback loop for whole being and wellness within. It is a constant flow if we let it.

We can create a circle of trust in our life and take this into other environments. Collect your anchors, breathe them in and absorb the strength that they give you. Take this strength with you into the circle, and deposit it there. Put all your anchor deposits into the circle, then step into the circle and draw on this incredible collection of life-giving resources. Project this into the future by noticing how different you will be when using this amazing cache of resource. The circle can go with you anywhere. Notice what happens when you use this.

Here's something to do now:

Imagine times and places when having this resource will be critical. How different will you be as a result of using this circle of trust?

Practice and apply:

Understanding yourself, your wants and aversions, your goals and disappointments is the key to growth as a human being. Knowing what you don't want is the first step to creating what you do want. Use your circle of trust to build a bigger platform for life. It's the energy we can mainline into, draw from, be inspired by. We can share it, be given it, lead others to it, or be led. All you need is a signpost to your destination.

Be the Best You Can Be

If you desire to be the best you can be, it is good to know how you can change and where the journey of transformation will lead. This ability to transform will allow you to travel faster and with greater pleasure. You can explore whether your current values and beliefs are consistent with your history. You may well be in a point of your life right now where change is imminent, and by looking at your current values and beliefs, and being able to visualise what you want to be as this will enable you to keep your vision in front of mind.

You can also apply these principles

- Think positively - the more you do this, the more you will naturally achieve. What the mind thinks, life proves. Share and seek to find a stronger balance for life. Always tell yourself you are better than you are.
- Think of the big picture and the detail will find its place. Your memories and experiences belong to you. If they don't equate with your bigger vision, change them. It is your privilege.
- Seek to learn from others, and do not fear all the bad things, because they may inspire you to become better. Fill your life with positive influences and be wise enough to know that your friends are often a mirror of yourself. If you look into that mirror and don't like what you see, change them.
- Find time to relax. You will achieve more if you are calm and focused. Allow space to listen to what is going on inside your body. It will use its ability to recharge, refocus and recreate what you need.

- Remember to be who you are instead of who you are not, especially when you are tempted to fall back into the ways you are now moving away from.

Can you teach yourself and others how to 'let go and move on'?

Here's something to do now:

Imagine yourself healing with love, breathing love and being the love you aspire to give and receive. What new skills do you have as part of your armoury? Are you calm, confident and communicating effectively?

Practice and apply:

By opening your circle of trust you will find deeper meaning as you draw closer to the person you are. Remember, your mind and body are a linked system and your behaviour is determined by making the best choice available. It is dependent on the circumstance, not your identity. Any mountain can be conquered if the climb is broken down into small steps. Underpinning every act is a positive intention. Just notice what it is.

Story Time

You can be far more effective when you use the language patterns that anticipate what you want, rather than those you don't want. You can use your words and tone of voice to develop your own stories and make them engaging to listen to. You can also rewrite old stories and choose how you tell them, so that you feel happy and fulfilled.

Next time you have a difference of opinion with someone, use this technique.

To increase bonding, agree to disagree on the issue that separates you. Do it gently. Discuss how you have done this for about 5 minutes and notice what occurs. Then, maintaining this level of rapport, look the other person in the eyes and understand the bond between you. Enjoy this sensation of gently disagreeing and doing so with respect and affection.

What have you learnt and where could you apply this?

Stories can immediately build a bond and it's good to know that when we talk to the life inside we are telling a story. Tell the story of your life and feel into all parts of the unfolding adventure.

You can use your words powerfully to influence ourselves and others through storytelling. Here are some key tips:

- **Cover all bases:** This pattern is useful and can be tailored to particular circumstances. Use the approach of saying, 'I know that we have done this before, and I know some love it and some would rather be elsewhere. Maybe today we could do something new, whatever interests you...'

- **Yes, Yes, Yes Set**: By receiving three undeniable facts in a row the mind is likely to take the next statement as true as well. For example: 'It's time to get up, (yes) we have around 30 minutes to be ready, (yes) so now would be a good time to start my morning routines and rituals and set myself up for the day, (yes).

Words to use with care:

Some words should be used with caution as it is possible to interpret them to mean the opposite of what is intended.

- 'If' always implies the possibility of choice, so avoid it, unless you want to allow choice.
- 'Try to' might mean fail. So if success is what you want from someone else, use another word.
- 'But' always negates what has just been said. Saying 'but' after another person's statement, could lead to defensiveness on the other person's part.
- 'Don't' the truth is, we can't 'not think of something', we will hear the 'don't' command and will immediately visualise doing exactly what you have said don't do. It's then a short step to doing what you want to achieve.

To get to a happy ever after, start by listing all the things you are grateful for. Focus on them in your mind, visualise them, and give them each a title to easily draw them from your mind i.e. family, home, health. Make sure you associate each word with a clear detailed vision.

This can help know your 'YES' from your 'NO'. Teaching and explaining what 'I want' rather than the 'don't do's' really can help.

Here's something to do now:

Sit down next to someone. Tell them a story that takes them to a wonderful place full of aspiration, hope and beauty. Instead of lots of facts and details, focus on the journey and success.

Practice and apply:

We can't help communicating. Every moment of every day we reach out to others, to the future and places deep within. In all these places there is no such thing as opposition, only lack of rapport. Within the dance of life, use your communication skills to tell your story, all of it, and add the meaning that you want. Pause and think about what you believe and understand the truth that comes from every pore of you.

It will change the way you dance and the messages you convey. You need not elaborate on the message that is pouring from you. Once you have registered your truth with the world outside, the language of your whole being will be clear, simple and compelling. It is your unique conversation with the world and if you believe that conversation is worth having then you will always have an audience.

Your relationship with the world outside starts on the inside. Take a moment to talk to the life within. Gently murmur: 'Born to LOVE. I can fulfil my true purpose and heal with love; love is the only happiness in the world. Because: I am free to change, and change means I will act towards my destiny.'

Always Be KIND. Always be YOU.

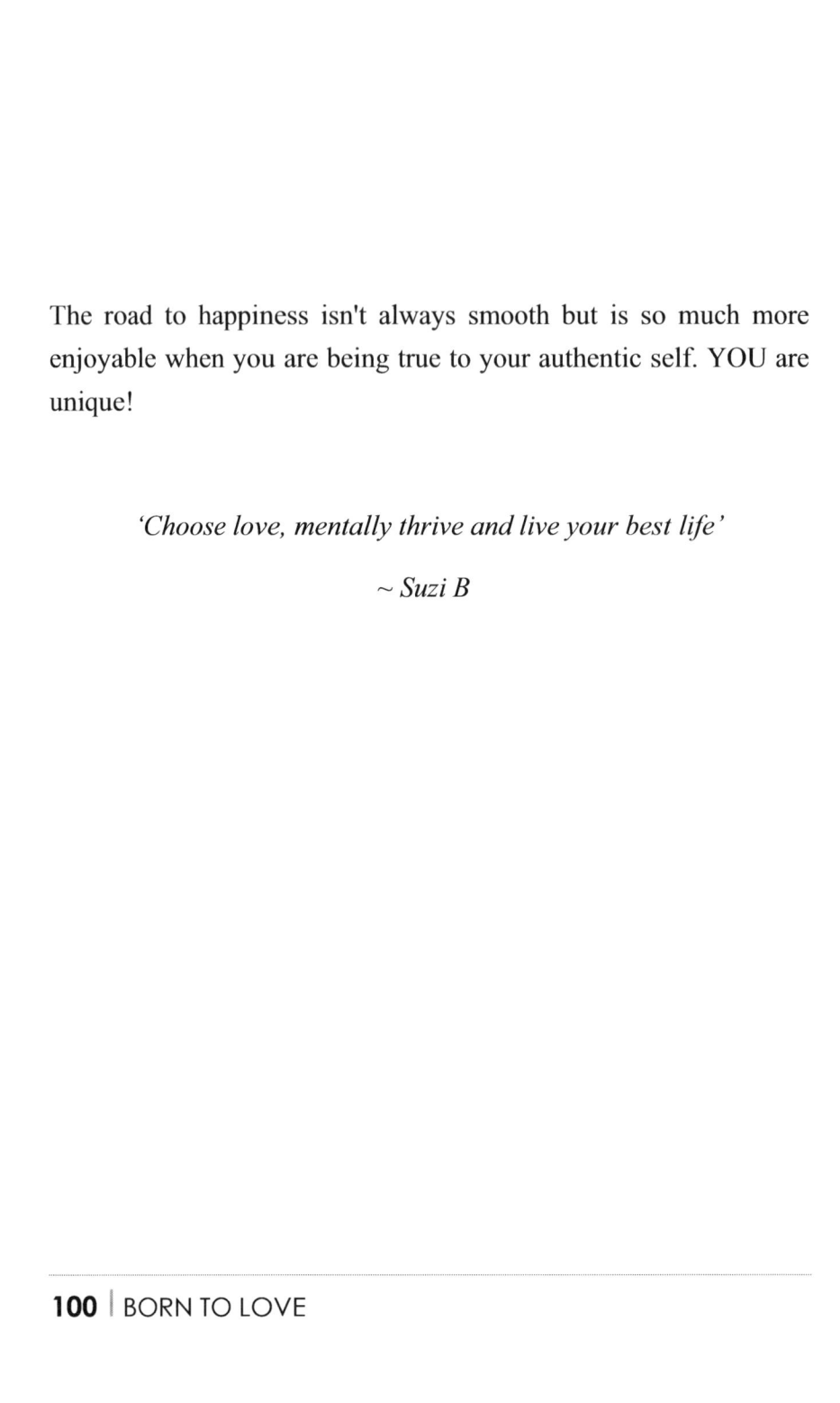

The road to happiness isn't always smooth but is so much more enjoyable when you are being true to your authentic self. YOU are unique!

'Choose love, mentally thrive and live your best life'

~ Suzi B

LOVE, LEARN, CONNECT

Now go and change the world, one person at a time, starting with you and the life you aspire to live.

'Born to love, of course, if that's what you want'

~ Suzi B

www.suzib.co.uk. All rights reserved. No part of this publishing may be reproduced or transmitted in any form or by any means, electronic or mechanical, including photocopy, recording of any information storage and retrieval system, without permission in writing from the publisher.

Copyright: Unauthorised copying, public performance (except for training) and broadcasting of this book is strictly prohibited. Produced, distributed by~SuziB.

Printed in Great Britain
by Amazon